Michael M. Dediu

Grand Canal - Venice
A new photographic viewpoint

A short presentation with many photos

DERC Publishing House
Tewksbury (Boston), Massachusetts, U. S. A.

Copyright ©2013 by Michael M. Dediu

All rights reserved

Published and printed in the
United States of America

Library of Congress Cataloging in Publication Data

Dediu, Michael M.

Grand Canal - Venice – a new photographic viewpoint

ISBN-13: 978-0981730073
ISBN-10: 0981730078

1-890034831

Preface

Many places are famous in Venice, but the Grand Canal has a special significance, and for this reason I dedicated most of this book to the Canal Grande, with a new photographic viewpoint.

The over 170 photos, taken in October 2012, show a delightful diversity of Palazzi, each one with an impressive personality and history.

I want to thank my wife Sophia for her help.

Our distinguished readers will be enchanted to view the splendors of the Grand Canal of Venezia, with detailed descriptions, and thus will certainly understand why Marco Polo, Bellini, Titian, Tintoretto, Veronese, Tiepolo, Canaletto, Palladio, Monteverdi, Vivaldi and many others - who lived and worked in Venezia – admired so much this unbelievable Canal Grande.

Michael M. Dediu, Ph. D.
U. S. A.

Michael M. Dediu is the author of these other books (which can be found on Amazon.com):

1. Aphorisms and quotations – with examples and explanations
2. Axioms, aphorisms and quotations – with examples and explanations
3. 100 Great Personalities and their Quotations
4. Professor Petre P. Teodorescu – A Great Mathematician and Engineer
5. Professor Ioan Goia – A Dedicated Engineering Professor
6. Venice (Venezia) – a new perspective. A short presentation with photographs
7. La Serenissima (Venice) - a new photographic perspective. A short presentation with many photos

Michael M. Dediu is the editor of these books (also on Amazon.com):

1. Sophia Dediu: The life and its torrents – Ana. In Europe around 1920
2. Proceedings of COMAT 2012
3. Adolf Shvedchikov: I am an eternal child of spring – poems in English, Italian, French, German, Spanish and Russian
4. Adolf Shvedchikov: Life's Enigma – poems in English, Italian and Russian
5. Adolf Shvedchikov: Everyone wants to be HAPPY – poems in English, Spanish and Russian
6. Adolf Shvedchikov: My Life, My Love – poems in English, Italian and Russian
7. Adolf Shvedchikov: I am the gardener of love – poems in English and Russian
8. Adolf Shvedchikov: Amaretta di Saronno – poems in English and Russian
9. Adolf Shvedchikov: A Russian Rediscovers America

Table of Contents

Table of Contents 5

Chapter 1. Piazza San Marco 7

Chapter 2. Lido di Venezia 13

Chapter 3. Venezia 19

Chapter 4. Canal Grande 35

Chapter 5. Ponte di Rialto 93

Chapter 6. General views 99

Grand Canal - Venice – a new photographic viewpoint

Chapter 1. Piazza San Marco

Il Torre dell'Orologio (the Clock Tower) is on the north side of the Piazza San Marco, and was completed in 1499. The bell was cast at the Arsenal in 1497. The winged lion of Venice is below the bell.

The west façade of the Palazzo Ducale (Doge's Palace), 1420.

Center right up detail of the west façade of the Basilica San Marco (1071). The four Greek horses, from the Hippodrome of Constantinople, installed in 1254, can be seen in center left.

Center right up detail of the west façade of the Basilica San Marco (1071), with statues of Theological and Cardinal Virtues.

The south façade of the Palazzo Ducale (1420) on Riva degli Schiavoni.

Il Torre dell'Orologio (the Clock Tower) is on the north side of the Piazza San Marco (1499). On the top of the Torre there are two big bronze statues, hinged at the waist, which strike the hours on the bell. One is old and the other young and they are wearing sheepskins. The Winged Lion of Venice is below the bell and holds the book quoting "Pax Tibi Marce Evangelista Meus" (Peace to you Mark my evangelist).

Center right detail of the west façade of the Basilica San Marco (1071). The central doorway (left) has Romanesque carvings.

Palazzo Giustinian (left), Piazza San Marco (center), Palazzo Ducale (center-right), seen from the east end of Canal Grande.

The west and south façades of Palazzo Ducale (1420), Palazzo dei Prigioni (right), on the street Riva degli Schiavoni.

Procuratie Vecchie (left), the south façade of the Basilica di San Marco (center), and the west façade of Palazzo Ducale (right).

Chapter 2. Lido di Venezia

A big historic building (now hotel), featuring Baroque-style decor and a façade with majolica tiles. It is about 400 m from the beach, 300 m from the vaporetto water bus stop, and it is located on Granviale Santa Maria Elisabetta in Lido di Venezia, which is an island, 11 km long, located east of Venice, forming a barrier between Venice and the Adriatic Sea. It has about 20,000 residents. At the north end there is the main entrance to the Laguna Veneto for ships. Since 1053 in the northern part there is a Benedictine abbey. In the south, Malamocco was one of the main centres of the Lagoon until the twelfth century. In the seventeenth century, in the centre of Lido, a new town began to grow around the church of Santa Maria Elisabetta.

Granviale Santa Maria Elisabetta (right) and Via Negroponte (left)

The east end of Granviale Santa Maria Elisabetta at Lungomare Gabriele D'Annunzio (left), Lungomare G. Marconi (right), with the beach and Adriatic Sea visible in the center.

On Granviale Santa Maria Elisabetta, 300 m from the beach.

The sandy beach by the Adriatic Sea, 50 m from the east end of Granviale Santa Maria Elisabetta.

The sandy beach by the Adriatic Sea, near Granviale Santa Maria Elisabetta.

The vaporetto stop near the west end of Granviale Santa Maria Elisabetta.

The sandy beach by the Adriatic Sea.

The modern vaporetto stop near the west end of Granviale Santa Maria Elisabetta.

Grand Canal - Venice – a new photographic viewpoint

Chapter 3. Venezia

Monumento Vittorio Emanuele II (1820 – 1878), on Riva degli Schiavoni, near San Zaccaria vaporetti fermata, with Londra Palace hotel (left), 250 m east from Piazza San Marco.

Piazza San Marco with il Campanile, Palazzo Ducale (center), and other buildings on Riva degli Schiavoni (south of Venice).

Monumento Vittorio Emanuele II (1820 – 1878), on Riva degli Schiavoni, near San Zaccaria vaporetti fermata, between Rio del Vin and Rio dei Greci..

Palazzo Giustinian (second from left), Piazza San Marco with il Campanile, Palazzo Ducale (center), seen from Canal Grande.

Lanterna di Marco Polo at the corner of Marzaria San Salvador (center) with Calle dei Monti delle Ballotte di San Marco (1884).

Piazza San Marco with il Campanile, Palazzo Ducale (center), seen from Canal Grande.

Piazza San Marco with il Campanile, Giardini Reali (center), Palazzo Ducale (right), seen from Bacino di San Marco.

Giardini Reali (left), Libreria Sansoviniana, Piazza San Marco with il Campanile, Palazzo Ducale (center), from Bacino di San Marco.

The cruise ship Queen Elizabeth, from Hamilton, a new modern ocean liner, in the Port of Venice (west of Venice).

Giardini Reali (left), Libreria Sansoviniana, Piazza San Marco with il Campanile, Palazzo Ducale (center), from Bacino di San Marco.

The Crystal Serenity cruise ship and other two smaller cruise ships in Porto di Venezia.

Grand Canal - Venice – a new photographic viewpoint   25

The cruise ship Queen Elizabeth, from Hamilton, and other two smaller cruise ships in Porto di Venezia (west of Venice).

The Crystal Serenity cruise ship and a tugboat in Porto di Venezia, at the west end of Canale della Giudecca (south of Venice).

26   Grand Canal - Venice – a new photographic viewpoint

The west end of Canale della Giudecca, with buildings on the south side of the south bank of Canal Grande (south of Venice).

Stazione Marittima with the Crystal Serenity cruise ship (left) and other small boats, at the west end of Canale della Giudecca.

The west end of Canale della Giudecca, with buildings on the north side of Canale della Giudecca (south of Venice).

Stazione Marittima with the Crystal Serenity cruise ship (left) and other small boats, at the west end of Canale della Giudecca.

The west end of Canale della Giudecca, with buildings on the north side of this Canale, and la Chiesa di San Angelo Raffaele (right).

Buildings on Fondamenta Beata Giuliana di Collalto, on the north side of Sacca Fisola Island, south bank of Canale della Giudecca.

Terminal S. Basilio in the Port of Venice, in the back the churches San Angelo Raffaele (center left) and San Sebastiano (center).

San Sebastiano church (left), Rio di San Sebastiano (center), Palazzo Molin (right) on Fondamenta Zattere Al Ponte Lungo.

Palazzo Molin (right) on Fondamenta Zattere Al Ponte Lungo, on the north bank of Canale della Giudecca, south of Venice.

Beautiful houses on Fondamenta Zattere Al Ponte Lungo, on the north bank of Canale della Giudecca, south of Venice.

Palazzini on Fondamenta Zattere Al Ponte Lungo, on the north bank of Canale della Giudecca, with Chiesa di Ognissanti (back).

Biblioteca Servizio Didattico Universita Ca' Foscati (red), on Fondamenta Zattere Al Ponte Lungo, north Canale della Giudecca.

Palazzini on Fondamenta Zattere Al Ponte Lungo, on the north bank of Canale della Giudecca, with a statue on the white house.

Palazzo Molin (right) and other palazzini on Fondamenta Zattere Al Ponte Lungo, on the north bank of Canale della Giudecca.

Palazzo Clary (left) on Fondamenta Zattere Al Ponte Lungo, on the north bank of Canale della Giudecca, near Ponte Lungo (right).

Nice houses on Fondamenta Zattere ai Gesuati, on the north bank of Canale della Giudecca, near Ponte Lungo (left).

Ponte Lungo over Rio di San Trovaso, with la Chiesa di San Trovaso (right), on the north bank of Canale della Giudecca.

Nice buildings and a restaurant on Fondamenta Zattere ai Gesuati, on the north bank of Canale della Giudecca, near Ponte Lungo.

Chapter 4. Canal Grande

Palazzo Querini (right), Canale di Cannaregio (center-right), Palazzo Labia (center-right), Chiesa San Geremia (center-left), 350 m east from the Venice Santa Lucia Train Station, 1.3 km from the west end of the Canal, and 2.6 km from Piazza San Marco.

Ponte e Chiesa degli Scalzi and Palazzo Calbo-Crotta (left)

Chiesa degli Scalzi (the church of Santa Maria di Nazareth) was built by Baltassarre Longhena in 1654, and the façade made by Giuseppe Sardi is the only one in Venice built with Carrara marble.

Venice Santa Lucia Train Station (left), la Chiesa di San Simeon Piccolo (center-right).

Giardino e Palazzo Papadopoli (right), bridge over Rio del Malcanton (left), and houses across the Santa Lucia Train Station.

Chiesa di San Simeon Piccolo (left), Palazzo Emo-Diedo (center), and other houses across the Santa Lucia Train Station.

Chiesa di San Simeon Piccolo (right), Palazzo Adoldo (center), across the Santa Lucia Train Station.

Grand Canal - Venice – a new photographic viewpoint 39

Fermata Ferrovia (left), Palazzo Calbo-Crotta (left), Chiesa San Geremia (back), Ponte degli Scalzi (bridge of the barefoot, 1934).

Chiesa S. Simeon Piccolo (right), Palazzi Adoldo (center), Foscari.

Chiesa degli Scalzi and Palazzo Calbo-Crotta (left), north bank

Chiesa di San Simeon Piccolo (left, 1738) on Fondamenta San Simeon Piccolo, on the south bank of the Canal Grande, across the Canal Grande from the Venice Santa Lucia railway station.

Palazzo Emo-Diedo (right) on Fondamenta San Simeon Piccolo, across the Canal Grande from the Santa Lucia railway station.

Near Fermata Ferrovia (left), Ponte degli Scalzi (left, 1934), Palazzi Foscari (center-right), Adoldo (right).

42   Grand Canal - Venice – a new photographic viewpoint

Ponte and Chiesa degli Scalzi, and Palazzo Calbo-Crotta (left), and other nice houses on the north bank of Canal Grande

The north half of Ponte degli Scalzi (bridge of the barefoot, 1934), Palazzo Calbo-Crotta (center-left), Chiesa San Geremia (back).

Fermata Ferrovia (left), Palazzo Calbo-Crotta (left), Chiesa San Geremia (back), Ponte degli Scalzi (bridge of the barefoot, 1934).

Palazzi Priuli-Bon (left) and Ca' Tron (center & right) with Facolta di Pianificazione Urbanistica e Territoriale, 700 m east from Scalzi

Ponte degli Scalzi (left, 1934), Chiesa degli Scalzi (right, 1654), and Fermata Ferrovia (down).

From under Ponte degli Scalzi, Palazzo Calbo-Crotta (white), and Fermata Ferrovia.

Palazzo Adoldo (left), Chiesa di San Simeon Piccolo (center, 1738), across the Canal Grande from the Santa Lucia train station.

Beautiful houses with a garden, on the south bank of Canal Grande, near Rio Marin (right), 40 m east of Ponte degli Scalzi.

Beautiful house (now hotel), on the south bank of Canal Grande, 80 m east of Ponte degli Scalzi.

Palazzo Gritti (left) and another nice house on the south bank of Canal Grande, 120 m east of Ponte degli Scalzi.

Fermata Riva di Biasio (left), Palazzi Dona-Balbi (left), Corner (center-left) and Gritti (center), 220 m east of Ponte degli Scalzi.

Palazzo Flangini (right) and other palazzini on the north bank of Canal Grande, 220 m east of Ponte degli Scalzi.

48 Grand Canal - Venice – a new photographic viewpoint

Palazzi Querini (left), Contarini (center) and Gritti (center-right), on the north bank, 320 m east of Ponte degli Scalzi

Palazzo Giovanelli (right) and other houses on the south bank of Canal Grande, 350 m east of Ponte degli Scalzi (ePS).

Chiesa San Geremia (left), Canale di Cannaregio (center), Palazzi Emo (center-right) and Querini (right), north bank, 230 m ePS.

Palazzi Gritti (left) and Vendramin Calergi (right big), 400 m ePS.

Fondaco di Turchi (left) with Museo di Storia Naturale, south bank, 500 m east of Ponte degli Scalzi (ePS).

Palazzo Belloni Battagia (left) and an administrative building (right), south bank, 530 m east of Ponte degli Scalzi (ePS).

Palazzo Flangini (center) and Chiesa San Geremia (right), north bank, 200 m east of Ponte degli Scalzi (ePS).

Palazzi Emo (left), Querini (center), Contarini (center-right) and Gritti (right), north bank, 300 m east of Ponte degli Scalzi

Ponte and Chiesa degli Scalzi (left), Palazzo Calbo-Crotta (center-left), and other nice houses on the north bank of the Canal Grande.

Palazzi Contarini (left), Gritti (center) and Vendramin Calergi (right), north bank, 340 m east of Ponte degli Scalzi.

Palazzo Calbo-Crotta (left), and other nice houses on the north bank of the Canal Grande, 20 m east of Ponte degli Scalzi (ePS).

Fondaco di Turchi with Museo di Storia Naturale, on the south bank of the Canal Grande, 500 m east of Ponte degli Scalzi (ePS).

54   Grand Canal - Venice – a new photographic viewpoint

Palazzi Belloni Battagia (right) and Ca' Tron (center-left) with Rio Ca' Tron between them, 370 m east of Ponte degli Scalzi (ePS).

Palazzi Ca' Tron (right), Priuli-Bon (center), Foscarini-Giovanelli

Grand Canal - Venice – a new photographic viewpoint

Palazzi Erizzo (left), Soranzo (center) and Emo (right), on the north bank, 400 m east of Ponte degli Scalzi (ePS).

Palazzo Molin (left and center) on the north bank of Canal Grande, 420 m east of Ponte degli Scalzi (ePS).

Ca' Pesaro (right) with Galleria d'Arte Moderna, Palazzi Dona (next) and Corner di Regina (big left), south bank, 500 m ePS.

Palazzo Buldu (center and right), on the north bank of Canal Grande, 500 m east of Ponte degli Scalzi (ePS).

Palazzo Fontana, with Rio di San Felice (left), on the north bank of the Canal Grande, 530 m east of Ponte degli Scalzi (ePS).

Palazzo Sagredo (right), on the north bank of the Canal Grande, 580 m east of Ponte degli Scalzi (ePS).

58   Grand Canal - Venice – a new photographic viewpoint

Palazzi Fontana (left), Ca' D'Oro (center-right) and Sagredo (right), north bank, 550 m east of Ponte degli Scalzi (ePS).

Palazzi Sagredo (left), Foscari (center) and Michiel di Colonne (big right), north bank, 600 m east of Ponte degli Scalzi (ePS).

Palazzi Michiel di Colonne (left) and Mangilli (center-right), north bank, 630 m east of Ponte degli Scalzi (ePS).

Rio di San Giovanni Crisostomo (center-left) with nice houses around, north bank, 200 m west of Ponte Rialto.

Palazzo Molin (left) and other nice houses on the north bank of the Canal Grande, 450 m east of Ponte degli Scalzi (ePS).

Palazzo Fontana (right) with Rio di San Felice (next), on the north bank of the Canal Grande, 520 m east of Ponte degli Scalzi (ePS).

Palazzi Ca' D'Oro (center-right) and Sagredo (right), north bank, 570 m east of Ponte degli Scalzi (ePS).

Palazzo Michiel di Colonne (center-right), north bank, 630 m ePS.

Ca' D'Oro, north bank, 580 m east of Ponte degli Scalzi (ePS).

Palazzi Michiel di Colonne (left) and Mangilli (center and right), north bank, 650 m east of Ponte degli Scalzi (ePS).

Palazzo Civran (center-right) and other nice buildings, north bank, 100 m west of Ponte Rialto.

Beautiful houses on Fondamenta del Vin Castello, on the south bank of the Canal Grande, 50 m east of Ponte Rialto.

64 Grand Canal - Venice – a new photographic viewpoint

Ca' D'Oro (right) and a palazzo with statues built in 1766 (center), north bank, 580 m east of Ponte degli Scalzi.

Palazzo Civran (left) and Fondaco di Tedeschi (right), north bank, 30 m west of Ponte Rialto.

Palazzo Dolfin-Manin (right), Fermata Rialto, north bank, 30 m south from Ponte Rialto.

Beautiful houses on Fondamenta del Vin Castello, on the south bank of the Canal Grande, 50 m south of Ponte Rialto.

Palazzi Bembo (left) and Dandolo (center-left), Fermata Rialto (center), north bank, 130 m south of Ponte Rialto.

Palazzi Rava (center-left), Barzizza and Papadopoli (left tall), Fermata San Silvestro (left), 170 m south of Ponte Rialto..

Palazzi Loredan/Ca' Farsetti (left two, Municipio), Grimani (center-right tall), north bank, 250 m south of Ponte Rialto.

Palazzo Rava (center), on Fondamenta del Vin Castello, south bank, 250 m south of Ponte Rialto.

Fermata San Silvestro and Palazzo Barzizza (center and left), south bank, 300 m south of Ponte Rialto.

Palazzi Tron (left), Volpi (covered) and Benzon on the north bank of Canal Grande, 400 m south of Ponte Rialto.

Palazzi Bembo (left) and Dandolo (center-left), Fermata Rialto (center), north bank, 150 m south from Ponte Rialto.

Palazzo Dona on the south bank, 450 m south from Ponte Rialto.

Grand Canal - Venice – a new photographic viewpoint

Palazzi Loredan/Ca' Farsetti (left) and Grimani (center tall) on the north bank of Canal Grande, 270 m south from Ponte Rialto.

Palazzo Barzizza, south bank, 300 m south of Ponte Rialto.

Nice palazzo (center) near palazzo Papadopoli (left), south bank, 320 m south of Ponte Rialto.

Palazzi Bernardo (right), Querini (center-left), Grimani, Layard and Barbarigo (left), south bank 370 m south of Ponte Rialto (sPR)

72 Grand Canal - Venice – a new photographic viewpoint

Palazzi Mocenigo (center-left, north bank), Giustinian (center-right, south bank), Ca' Foscari and Balbi (right), 700 m sPR.

Palazzi Persigo (right, north bank), Marcello di Leoni (center), Dandolo-Paolucci (center-left), Civran-Grimani (left), 700 m sPR..

Palazzi Layard (right), Barbarigo (center and left), Pisani Mor (left), with Rio di San Polo (center), 500 m south of Rialto.

Fermata San Toma (right), Palazzi Civran-Grimani (right), Balbi (center- right), Ca' Foscari (center), Giustinian, Nani (left), 700 m

74 Grand Canal - Venice – a new photographic viewpoint

Palazzi Querini (left), Grimani (center), Layard (center-left) and Barbarigo (left), south bank, 470 m south of Ponte Rialto.

Palazzi Marcello di Leoni (center & right), Dandolo Paolucci (center-left), Civran-Grimani (left), Fermata San Toma (left), 660 m sR

Balbi (center- right, tall), Ca' Foscari (center-left), Giustinian (left), south bank, 740 m south of Ponte Rialto.

Palazzi Ca' Rezzonico (center), bridge over Rio di San Barnaba Contarini-Michiel (center-left) and Stern (left), 1.2 km west of SM

76   Grand Canal - Venice – a new photographic viewpoint

Palazzi Barbarigo (right), Pisani Mor (center), Tiepolo (center-left), Persogo (left), south bank, 520 m south of Ponte Rialto.

Palazzi Mocenigo (left, north bank), Ca' Rezzonico (center-left, south bank), Nani, Giustinian, Ca' Foscari and Balbi (right), 750 m

Fermata San Samuele (right), Chiesa di San Samuele (center, Palazzo Grassi (left), north bank, 1.15 km west of San Marco.

Palazzo Giustinian-Lolin (center-left, north bank), Ponte dell'Accademia (center) and Accademia (right, south bank), 900 m

Palazzo Giustinian-Lolin (left) and a lovely palazzino on the north bank, near Ponte dell'Accademia, 870 m west of Piazza San Marco

The north half of Ponte dell'Accademia, Palazzo Cavalli Franchetti (center), Chiesa Santa Maria della Salute (back), 850 m wSM.

Palazzi Ca' Rezzonico (left), Nani (center-left), Giustinian, Ca' Foscari and Rio Ca' Foscari (right), south bank, 800 m sPR.

Fermata San Samuele and reflected in windows Palazzi Ca' Rezzonico (left), Contarini-Michiel (center) and Stern (right).

Ponte dell'Accademia, Palazzo Cavalli Franchetti (left), Chiesa Santa Maria della Salute (back), 830 m west of Piazza San Marco.

Palazzi Barbaro (left), Pisani (center-right), Stecchini and Corner (right), north bank, 720 m west of Piazza San Marco.

Grand Canal - Venice – a new photographic viewpoint   81

The north end of Ponte dell'Accademia (right) and nice houses on the north bank of Cana Grande, 850 m west of Piazza San Marco.

Palazzi Cavalli Franchetti (center) and Barbaro, near Ponte dell'Accademia, north bank, 750 m west of Piazza San Marco.

Palazzi Nani (left), Giustinian (center& left), Ca' Foscari (right), south bank, 820 m south of Ponte Rialto.

Nice houses on the north bank of Canal Grande, 1.1 km west from Piazza San Marco.

Grand Canal - Venice – a new photographic viewpoint   83

Ponte dell'Accademia, Palazzo Cavalli Franchetti (left), Chiesa Santa Maria della Salute (back), 850 m west of Piazza San Marco.

The north end of Ponte dell'Accademia (right) and nice houses on the north bank of Cana Grande, 850 m west of Piazza San Marco.

84 Grand Canal - Venice – a new photographic viewpoint

Palazzi Barbarigo (right), Da Mula (center-left), Centani and Venier dei Leoni (left), south bank, 700 m west of San Marco.

Palazzi Dario (right, covered), and Genovese (center-left) and Chiesa Santa Maria della Salute (back), 550 m west of San Marco.

Palazzi Cavalli Franchetti (left) and Barbaro (center), near Ponte dell'Accademia, north bank, 720 m west of Piazza San Marco.

Palazzi Barbarigo (right), Da Mula (center), and Centani (center-left), on the south bank of Canal Grande, 670 m west of Piazza San Marco

Palazzi Gritti (center) and Ferrofini (center-right), north bank, 430 m west of Piazza San Marco.

Palazzo Genovese (center), south bank of Canal Grande, 420 m west of Piazza San Marco.

Palazzi Gritti (left), Ferrofini (center-left) and Contarini Fasan (center), north bank, 380 m west of Piazza San Marco.

Chiesa Santa Maria della Salute, 350 m west of Piazza San Marco.

Palazzo Corner (Ca' Granda, Prefettura), north bank, 600 m west of Piazza San Marco.

Palazzi Ferrofini (left) and Contarini Fasan (center-right), north bank, 360 m west of Piazza San Marco

Grand Canal - Venice – a new photographic viewpoint 89

Dogana da Mar (center) on the eastern tip of the south bank of Canal Grande, 260 m south-west from Piazza San Marco.

Palazzi Treves de Bonfili (left) and Giustinian (center), north bank, 230 m west of Piazza San Marco.

Palazzi Contarini Fasan (left), Tiepolo (center-right) and Treves de Bonfili (right), north bank, 350 m west of Piazza San Marco.

Palazzo Giustinian (second from left), with il Campanile in the back, at the east exit of the Canal Grande.

Procuratie Nuove (right), Fermata San Marco (center-right), Giardini Reali (right), Chiesa San Fantin (in the back, near Teatro La Fenice), Capitano di Porto (center), Palazzo Giustinian (center-left), at the east entrance in the Canal Grande.

Chapter 5. Ponte di Rialto

Ponte di Rialto (1588 – 1591) with Fermata Rialto (right), seen from south.

Ponte di Rialto, with gondole, seen from north.

The east end of Ponte di Rialto seen from north.

The west end of Ponte di Rialto seen from north

Under the Ponte di Rialto, seen from north, with Fermata Rialto (center-right).

96 Grand Canal - Venice – a new photographic viewpoint

The west end of Ponte di Rialto, seen from north

Under the Ponte di Rialto, seen from north, with Fermata Rialto (center), and palazzi on the north bank of Canal Grande.

Exiting from under the Ponte di Rialto, seen from north, with houses on the south bank of Canal Grande

Grand Canal - Venice – a new photographic viewpoint

Chapter 6. General views

Capitano di Porto (left), Giardini Reali (center-left), Il Campanile from Piazza San Marco, Libreria Sansoviniana (center-left), Palazzo Ducale (center), and Riva degli Schiavoni on which are splendid houses on the south side of Venezia.

Via Liberta, the freeway SS11 which connects Venezia (on the right) with the mainland (on the left), seen from the west end of the Canal Grande.

The central left side of the cruise ship Queen Elizabeth in Porto di Venezia, on the west side of Venice.

The cruise ship Crystal Serenity (right) in Porto di Venezia.

Giardini Reali (left), Il Campanile from Piazza San Marco, Libreria Sansoviniana (center-left), Palazzo Ducale (center).

The cruise ship Queen Elizabeth in Porto di Venezia, on the west side of Venice.

Giardini Reali (left), Il Campanile from Piazza San Marco, Libreria Sansoviniana (center), and Palazzo Ducale (right).

The cruise ship Queen Elizabeth in Porto di Venezia.

The cruise ship Queen Elizabeth (left) and other two cruise liners in Porto di Venezia, on the west side of Venice

The cruise ship Crystal Serenity (right) in Porto di Venezia, seen from the west end of Canale della Giudecca.

The cruise ship Crystal Serenity (left) in Porto di Venezia, seen from the west end of Canale di Giudecca.

The north bank of Canale della Giudecca near its west end.

106   Grand Canal - Venice – a new photographic viewpoint

The cruise ship Crystal Serenity (left) and a nice yacht in Porto di Venezia, seen from the west end of Canale della Giudecca.

Terminal San Basilio of the Port of Venice, on the north bank of Canale della Giudecca at its west end.

CPSIA information can be obtained
at www.ICGtesting.com
Printed in the USA
LVIC04n1913160114
369730LV00008BA/58